To Chris,
Steve, Maddy +
Abby, May you find
Holiness in the
Ordinary.

‏בברכה‎ 8/15/17

Rabbi G.

Have You Heard?

A Child's Introduction to the Ten Commandments

Rabbi Jeffrey Glickman | Illustrated by Eric Krackow

Schiffer Publishing Ltd

4880 Lower Valley Road • Atglen, PA 19310

Other Schiffer Books on Related Subjects:

The Legend of Papa Balloon,
C.R. McClure, 978-0-7643-4410-7

The Psalm® Cards: And Messages from the Psalms,
Rabbi Robert dos Santos Teixeira, LCSW, 978-0-7643-5191-4

Everyday MAGICK for Children of Earth-Based Spiritual Families,
Rayne Storm, 978-0-7643-4017-8

Designed by Justin Watkinson
Cover design by Brenda McCallum
Type set in DINEngschrift/Century Gothic/Minion Pro

ISBN: 978-0-7643-5395-6
Printed in China

Published by Schiffer Publishing, Ltd.
4880 Lower Valley Road
Atglen, PA 19310
Phone: (610) 593-1777; Fax: (610) 593-2002
E-mail: Info@schifferbooks.com
Web: www.schifferbooks.com

For our complete selection of fine books on this and related subjects, please visit
our website at www.schifferbooks.com. You may also write for a free catalog.

Schiffer Publishing's titles are available at special discounts for bulk purchases for
sales promotions or premiums. Special editions, including personalized covers,
corporate imprints, and excerpts, can be created in large quantities for special
needs. For more information, contact the publisher.

We are always looking for people to write books on new and related subjects.
If you have an idea for a book, please contact us at proposals@schifferbooks.com.

Dedicated to the
original author of the
Ten Commandments

Preface

We tell a story of Moses receiving the Ten Commandments at Mount Sinai over three thousand years ago. Whether or not this story actually happened, the world was changed by its telling. It is the first time a leader told the people that reading was a good thing— the first time a day of rest was mandated.

I firmly believe that this is a true story. This book is an attempt to make it more accessible to young people and their parents. The title, *Have You Heard?*, references the Hebrew name *Aseret Hadibrot*, or "The Spoken Ten." If God is reaching out to us through speaking, it is our role to hear.

The Ten Commandments emphasize values of integrity, community, and happiness in a loving voice. My goal is to show them here in an elegant way.

Each commandment is summarized with plain words. You can use these as seeds for the important values children need to be taught. The longer paragraphs for each commandment and the activities in the Appendix help you to grow these seeds.

The illustrator, Eric Krackow, is a brilliant and sensitive man who took these insights and made them much more than I had imagined with his engaging artwork.

It can be hard for parents to talk about religion. This book is your starting point for a journey of meaning, wonder, and holiness.

To share your own activities and experiences learning or teaching the Ten Commandments, visit www.TurnToTheWonderful.com

Have you heard?
God loves you.

God is much more than we are. God doesn't need to talk to us or care about us. But God talked to us when we were given the Ten Commandments. God does care about us, and these commandments make our life better. When you care about someone and want them to do well, that is a kind of love. A good mother and a good father care about us all the time. They do nice things for us and help us to do well. Even though God is much more than a good father and a good mother, we learn about how God loves us by the way our parents love us.

Have you heard?

What is made up isn't always real.

You can't see the wind, but you can feel it, and see the way it makes the leaves dance. God is like the wind. We can't see God, but we can see the things God has made and can feel God's love for us. The Ten Commandments tells us not to make a statue of what we think God looks like. Statues are made up. It can be confusing, because we think statues are real. But, they are just empty on the inside. It is hard to know what is real and what is pretend.

Have you heard?

Words are powerful, use them carefully.

You have a name. When that is called, your ears perk up. A name is a word—a powerful word. God also has a name; actually God has many names. When we call God's name, it gets God's special attention. It can be for good things, like praying for someone who is hurt to get better. It can also be used for bad things when we are mad. God's name is a word we should treat carefully. In fact, we should treat all words carefully. Words can hurt people. Words can be used to make people feel loved, can give people hope, and can make people feel appreciated. We are told that the most powerful muscle in our body is our tongue!

Have you heard?
Everything rests.

Breathing is both in and out. The better you blow out, the better you can breathe in. Life is like that. There is both doing and resting. The better you rest, the better you can run around, the better you can think clearly, the better you can care about things. People need rest. So do plants and animals. God told us that it is good to have one day each week where we don't work. We use that day not just to sleep, but to listen, to think about things that happened, and to say thank you.

Have you heard?
Your parents are a part of you.

The people who raise us give us lots of things. Parents teach us and guide us and shape us. The things we get from our parents stay with us our whole life. They are a part of who we are. Guess what? We are a part of who they are, too!

Have you heard?
Don't waste.

God made this world with lots and lots of wonderful things. Every one of them has a purpose. It is there for a reason, even if we don't know what the reason is. For instance, God made lots of different things we can eat, and these things all have different tastes. Each fruit is a present from God. God wants us to enjoy our life. If we kill something, we might never know why it was created. Destroying things for fun is a bad thing to do. That is wasting. God doesn't want us to waste.

Have you heard?
Promises are treasures.

When you say you are going to help, you become a partner with other people. They are trusting you and are counting on you to do what you say. This is the way to do big things that are difficult, things that no one could do by themselves. A stronger way of saying you are going to do something is to promise. The biggest promise many people make is to be married. A promise means you are going to try very hard to keep your word. If you break a promise, it can be sad. It changes the way people listen to your words. Try not to make too many promises. It is hard to care about too many treasures. If you keep a promise, the treasure grows and grows.

Have you heard?
Not everything is yours.

A giraffe is an amazing animal. Watching it sway as it walks is fascinating. And it has such beautiful eyes. You don't have to buy a giraffe and take it home. You can visit it at the zoo and appreciate how wonderful it is.

It is the same with flowers in the park or toys in your friend's closet.

If you take something which isn't yours, you are stealing. That hurts people and makes it hard for them to be your friend. It is a special treat when someone gives you something. We say thank you with our words and just by taking good care of that present.

Have you heard?
You can remember what you see.

There are wonderful things happening all around us. If you keep your eyes open and pay attention, you can find things that will make you say, "WOW!" It is good to see things. It is also good to remember what you see. And, it is nice to tell people about what you found so interesting. You don't have to make things up; the things you can see are amazing enough. Sometimes, people say they saw something when they didn't see it. This is not nice. People don't like to be fooled. There are plenty of amazing things, just look closely!

Have you heard?
Your house can be just fine.

The only happy people I know are people who are happy with what they have.

—Rabbi Jeffrey Glickman

Translation of the Ten Commandments

Some faith groups divide the Ten Commandments differently. Here is a new translation, true to the original Hebrew.

Exodus 20:2–13

I am Adonai, your God, who freed you from Egypt, from the house of slavery.

You should not have any other gods before Me. Do not make for yourself an image or likeness of anything in the heavens above or in the earth below or in the waters below the earth. Do not bow down to any of them and do not serve them. Because I am Adonai your God, a God with feelings, who remembers the sins of the parents through the children, grandchildren, and great grandchildren, but who loves with kindness thousands on behalf of those who love Me and keep My commandments.

Do not use the name of Adonai your God lightly, because Adonai will hold accountable anyone who treats God's name lightly.

Remember the Shabbat day for holiness. Six days you should work and take care of all your tasks. The seventh day is Shabbat to Adonai your God. Do not do any manner of work—you, your children, your workers, and any visitors you have living with you. Because in six days, Adonai made the heavens, the earth, the sea, and all that is in them, and rested on the seventh day. Because of this, God blessed the seventh day that it should be holy.

Make your father and mother a weighty part of your life in order that the days that you have on the land Adonai your God is giving you may be long.

Don't waste life.

Don't break marriage vows.

Don't take what isn't yours.

Don't tell something you didn't see.

Don't envy your neighbor's house. Don't envy your neighbor's spouse, worker, ox, donkey, or anything which belongs to your neighbor.

Appendix

The Title

We came to a mountain in the middle of the desert. After generations of slavery in Egypt, we gathered in freedom and God spoke to us. God told us important words. In the original language, Hebrew, these words are called *Aseret Hadibrot*, "The Spoken Ten." We know them as the Ten Commandments. Our job is to hear them. Actually, listening is one of the most important things we can do. That is why this book is called, *Have You Heard?*

What It Means to Be Commanded

> "Hitch your wagon to a star."
> –RALPH WALDO EMERSON

My grandmother used to say that. She meant that it is good to reach for something much bigger than you are.

Children are precious. If we treat them as though they are the most important things in the world, it is an obstacle for them to listen to others and to grow. If you are perfect, why try harder?

That is why religion is so important. We are told how small we are in the world. Yet, we are also told that God cares about us. "What is man that you are mindful of us?" (Psalm 8).

There is a reason these are called commandments and not, "Ten Suggestions," or "Tips for Life." The reason is because God has a greater wisdom than we will ever have. Knowing that God only wants good for us makes it easier for us to trust that we will grow when we follow these commandments. We don't need to know why. Picking and choosing which ones we will follow treats God like our peer.

Why is it often good for a parent to say, "Because I said so"?

Exploring variations of love. Loving pizza is different than loving soccer, which is different than loving your dog.

What is a food that you love?
> What does love mean?

What is a hobby that you love?
> What does love mean?

What is an animal that you love?
> What does love mean?

How can you tell that your parents love you?
> How can you show that you love them back?

Real and make believe. Did a rabbit and a tortoise really race? Why is the story told? It is the most told story in the world. Even though it is made up, is there anything true about it?

Words are powerful. What is something another person said that made you feel good? Words can do that. Was there anything someone said that made you feel bad?

Rest. Stretch your arms out sideways and hold them in the air. Can you keep them up for a minute? Two minutes? It is easy to do at first, but after a while, it gets very hard. We need to rest them before we can lift them again. It is good to work and play with all your energy. It is also good to recharge your energy by resting.

Parents. When good parents raise children, they fill them up with love. That love stays with them and makes their faces shine. It gives them love to share with other people. Your parents were children once. They were filled with love. The love they are giving to you, they got from people who loved them. That love is a big part of who you are. Can you see any ways that your parents are like your grandparents?

Making less waste. Did you know that paper towels come from trees? The tree is cut down, chewed up in a big machine, and pressed thin into paper. After you use it, it becomes trash, and people work hard to find a place to put the trash. If everyone uses more paper towels, we need to cut down more trees, and find places for more trash. After you wash your hands, can you dry them with only half a towel? How small a piece of paper towel can you use? It is good to use just what you need for paper towels, and for lots of other things. Can you think of anything else that you can use less of?

Power of promises. Imagine each wooden block made a promise to come together to build a tower. If one of the blocks on the bottom says, "I've changed my mind, and want to go," what would happen to the tower?

Stealing. Your school is creating class flags. Anyone can come up with ideas. You think a rainbow is a good idea because it needs every color, just like our class needs every person. At lunch, you tell another student your idea. That classmate says it is a great idea, one that they never thought of. When class resumes, that student tells the teacher about the rainbow flag and that it is their idea. How do you feel? Is this stealing?

Seeing. God wanted to talk to Moses. God could have used lightning to get Moses's attention. Instead, God made something small to see if Moses was good at looking around. It was a little bush with flames. Most people would have walked right by it, but Moses noticed it and stopped. Is God trying to talk to us now? Are there many little burning bushes all over the place that people walk right by? What is something you have noticed that other people didn't see? If you look back at the pictures in this book, you will find burning bushes all over!

Contentment. Long ago, someone said, "I cried because I had no shoes until I met a man who had no feet." What does this mean?

Helen Keller said, "Instead of comparing our lot with that of those who are more fortunate than we are, we should compare it with the lot of the great majority of our fellow men. It then appears that we are among the privileged." Even though her eyes and her ears didn't work, she was a beloved writer and teacher who found great joy in life.

Can you think of ten things you have that many people don't have?